One Month
of the
Well-Watered Life
Devotional

TODD L. SHULER

PRAISE FOR *ONE MONTH OF THE WELL-WATERED LIFE DEVOTIONAL*

"Many of the topics you focus on each day are things I have been facing in my own spiritual journey. At times, I felt as if you were in my head. The daily prayers are powerful. Thank you for the blessing you provided through the words you wrote. I am now a Todd Shuler fan and will be buying other books. God bless you!"
R. Espinal, FL

"*The Well-Watered Life* carefully explores our complex relationship to one of life's simplest elements. Todd Shuler's careful study of both the Old and New Testament reminds us that, while physical water is so precious that wars have been fought over it, having our spiritual thirst assuaged at the Well of Living Water is even more vital."
Dr. Samuel & Mrs. Rheba Drye, Founders, Destiny Life Ministries, International

"I know that everyone who reads this book will be blessed."
Ms. Yvonne Hurst, Salvation Army

ONE MONTH OF THE WELL-WATERED LIFE DEVOTIONAL

One Month of the Well-Watered Life by Todd Shuler
Published by City of God Publishing
(a division of Crown Global Corporation)
223 Wimbledon Place
Macon, GA 31211-6022

ISBN: 0988958945
ISBN-13: 978-0988958944

For Worldwide Distribution
Printed in the U.S.A.

This book and all other City of God Publishing books are available at Christian bookstores, online retailers, and distributors worldwide.

For more information, call (404) 939-0807
Or reach us on the Web:
www.cityofgodpublishing.com

TABLE OF CONTENTS

DEDICATION

To my lovely wife Evetta,
along with our kids Trevor, Philip and Lauren.

To the God of Abraham, Issac, Jacob
and our Lord and Savior Jesus Christ...

To the God of my matriarchs:
Ms. Octavia Hill Shuler (1905-2005)
and Ms. Henrietta Ava Lockett (1914-2003)...

To the God of my parents:
Bishop Allen J. Shuler, Sr. and Mrs. Sallie L. Shuler...

To the God of my siblings:
Allen Jr. (and wife Connie), Shena (and husband Tony), Serina and Dana

To so many others who have loved, encouraged, and prayed me
(in spite of myself) down through the years...

Most of all, to my Lord Jesus Christ; my Master, Savior, and King.
Thank you for giving your life for me and all those who will read this book,
believe in You and receive Your Promise of Rest now
and the *Well-Watered Life* - life eternal.

To You be the Glory, Dominion, and Power.
Forever and Amen!

ACKNOWLEDGMENTS

My heartfelt gratitude and thanks to all these wonderful people who helped me create One Month of the Well-Watered Life: Stacey Bass, Matt Blanchard, Renay Bloom, Bettye Burney, Robin Castro, Angela Cherry, Jake Cox, Tim Culbertson, Rheba Drye, Marcy Lewis Ellerbee, Brian Ezeike, Byron Fleming, Anne Gardner, Randy Groomes, Gwendolyn Harvey, Arnetta Hatten, Lynette Howard, Stan Hutchinson, Pamela James, LaConia Dean Jenkins, Schanea Kelly, Hope Latimore, John Leslie, June Saunders, Shena Manning (my twin sister), Charlie Merritt, Evette Mills, Carlos Miro, Eddie Murphy, Nwabu Okeiyi, Carolyn Roark, Darren Short, Karen Star, Jim Taylor, Remeka Turk, Tammy Walls, Andrea Walthour, David Williams, and Heather Wise.

INTRODUCTION

The World Health Organization says that stress is a global phenomenon in our fast-paced, hectic modern era. In fact, for all our cutting edge conveniences, people in medieval times actually worked less than we do because of the liturgical calendar that gave them many, many holy days (holidays) from work. Our modern, 365/24/7 work schedule and its attendant stresses are affecting our health—and not just our physical health.

When do we take time to nourish and replenish our souls? If our souls are dehydrated, things just don't go as smoothly, adding to more stress. We need to take some time, take our own holy days, at least for some period of time every day to refresh and replenish our spirits. During this time we rest in the Lord. We may rest in fellowship with like-minded friends or in peace and solitude. In this way, we recharge our spiritual batteries for the ongoing battle to stay as sane and sinless as possible in a fast-paced, demanding, and imperfect world.

Jesus validated the need to take rest when he told his busy disciples, "Let's go off by ourselves to a quiet place and rest awhile." He said this because there were so many people coming and going that Jesus and his apostles didn't even have time to eat (Mark 6:31 New Living Translation). Now the crowds didn't leave Jesus and his apostles alone in that instance; they followed him to the "remote place" (Mark 6:35 NLT) he and his apostles went to for privacy and rest, and Jesus performed the miracle of the loaves and the fishes. His resting time would have to wait in that instance, because the need of the people was so great. At the same time, his attempt to find respite from the work and the crowds shows that he knew the value of rest, recommended it, and sought it during busy times.

Hence, I offer to readers this devotional. This 31-day thought and prayer guide is a place to drink of the living water that can give your soul rest and peace and make everything fall into place. You'll have more time and energy to spend on the things that matter most; and the things that matter less will still get done, often more efficiently and effectively than when you were hectically and frantically trying to pursue your never-ending to-do list.

The devotional will cover such topics as learning to rest, the lost gift of the Holy Spirit, dealing with overload, resting in the midst of adversity, enjoying freedom from the need to perform, surrender, creating a home and worship environment where your soul can rest, and many other topics.

I offer you a month of drinking water from the well from which you will never go thirsty again. It is our hope that during and after 31 days of prayer and reflection you will enjoy the incomparable refreshment, rest, and respite of putting everything into the Lord's hands.

Take rest; the field that has rested gives a bountiful crop.
- Ovid

DAY 1 - REFRESHMENT AND REST IN THE LORD

In many ways, water represents life itself. That's why it is such a powerful symbol of the life of the spirit.

When we experience spiritual thirst, we may feel like crying out as David did: "As the deer longs for streams of water, so I long for you, O God. I thirst for God, the living God." (Psalm 42:1-2 NLT). David also likened the thirst for a relationship with God to physical thirst: "O God, you are my God; I earnestly search for you. My soul thirsts for you; my whole body longs for you in this parched and weary land where there is no water" (Psalm 63:1 NLT).

In times of spiritual thirst, we must not turn to our secular culture to slake the yearning. That is a "parched and weary land where there is no water." Rather, we should turn to the well of living water, Jesus, as He said, "Those who drink the water I give will never be thirsty again. It becomes a fresh, bubbling spring within them, giving them eternal life" (John 4:13 NLT).

Prayer

Lord, sometimes the world inside and out seems like a vast, barren desert. I feel weary and parched in my soul. So much of modern culture is illusion and chasing the wind. When my soul is thirsty, let me not turn to the temporary comforts of the world of secularism and sin, but let me turn to the well of living water that is Jesus the Christ. Let me rest in Him, for Jesus said, "Peace I leave with you, my peace I give unto you: not as the world giveth, give I unto you" (John 14:27 King James Version). Let me find rest, respite, and refreshment in Your presence, Your Will, and Your Word. Resting in You, I know I will never be weary or thirsty in my soul again. In Jesus' name I pray.

Devotional Notes & Scripture References

_____

_____

_____

_____

_____

_____

_____

_____

_____

_____

_____

_____

_____

_____

_____

_____

_____

_____

_____

_____

_____

_____

_____

_____

_____

Devotional Notes & Scripture References

_____

_____

_____

_____

_____

_____

_____

_____

_____

_____

_____

_____

_____

_____

_____

_____

_____

_____

_____

_____

_____

_____

_____

_____

_____

_____

DAY 2 - "COME TO ME"

Come to me, all of you who are weary and carry heavy burdens, and I will give you rest. - Matthew 11:28 NLT

Perhaps you are at a place of drought. Your life does not feel well-watered. You may feel like you are face down in the desert, mouth full of sand, too weary and worn out to go on. Sometimes we experience droughts of money, love, peace, friends, employment, or health. Sometimes a good day can go bad, ruined by something as simple as a hard drive crash. Sometimes we experience more serious crashes. What do you do when your finances, your marriage, or some important family relationship crashes? What do you do when your job or your reputation crashes? What should you do during a painful time of drought?

The great forefather of Israel, Isaac, went through many crises or crashes in his life. As was noted in *The Well-Watered Life*, when faced with the drought of his wife's infertility, Isaac prayed (Genesis 25:21 NLT) and the Lord answered Isaac's prayer abundantly, for Rebecca's fertility was within His will.

Jesus assured us that we can lay our burdens at His feet: "Come to me, all of you who are weary and carry heavy burdens, and I will give you rest" (Matthew 11:28, NLT). Let's do so.

Prayer

Lord, I am facing a drought in my life, and I am heavily burdened. The nature of the drought is (name your struggle). Please show me what responsibility I have, if any, in causing this drought. Show me where I need to repent and reform. Show me what I need to do to make Amen.ds to You and to those I may have harmed. I also ask that You would reveal to me whether this drought is part of Your will for me. Are You perhaps trying to teach me something through this suffering? If so, let me learn it well and thoroughly. Thank You that You care about me enough to rebuke me. I believe Your promises that You love me and have prepared for me a future and a hope in spite of my current drought or crisis. In Jesus' name I pray. Amen.

Devotional Notes & Scripture References

Devotional Notes & Scripture References

_____

_____

_____

_____

_____

_____

_____

_____

_____

_____

_____

_____

_____

_____

_____

_____

_____

_____

_____

_____

_____

DAY 3 - DON'T YOU MISS HIM?

King David hit the nail on the head when he described his problems as resulting from a lack of a relationship with God. He likened it to a thirst. Let's look at the classic King James Version of Psalm 42:1-2: "As the hart panteth after the water brooks, so panteth my soul after thee, O God. My soul thirsteth for God, for the living God: when shall I come and appear before God?"

David wasn't just spiritually thirsty—he was panting, like a running deer, pursued by an enemy, with its chest heaving and its tongue hanging out, yearning for a moment of safety when it could drink from a brook in peace. Like a hunted deer, David missed the peace and safety of God's presence.

Don't you miss Him? Don't you wish you could live in His Kingdom of justice, truth, goodness, and beauty? This system of things, the world as it is, is not God's kingdom. It is as if believers are living in a strange and foreign land, where the rules are unclear, unfair, and unsafe. If people and *the system* make your life seem like a breathless race to nowhere, no matter how hard you try, have peace. Have faith. There's a promise: "Blessed are they which do hunger and thirst after righteousness, for they shall be filled" (Matthew 5:6 KJV). You can be filled this moment with the love and peace of the Lord.

Prayer

Lord, I wish things were different in this world. There are dangers and temptations wherever I turn. When I come home to relax, I see on TV sex depicted as casual and the temptations of material goods. Grown-up movies are laced with profanity. Relationships are difficult. I long to live with You. I yearn to live in Your Kingdom, where kindness, honesty, justice, and love for humankind are rewarded. Help me through prayer to live in that place of peace in my heart, knowing that You are there, and knowing that You have my back against my pursuing enemy, Satan, and all the temptations of this world. In Jesus' name I pray.

Devotional Notes & Scripture References

_____

_____

_____

_____

_____

_____

_____

_____

_____

_____

_____

_____

_____

_____

_____

_____

_____

_____

_____

_____

_____

_____

Devotional Notes & Scripture References

_____

_____

_____

_____

_____

_____

_____

_____

_____

_____

_____

_____

_____

_____

_____

_____

_____

_____

_____

_____

_____

_____

_____

_____

_____

DAY 4 - LORD, I MADE A MISTAKE

We all make mistakes. We all miss the target from time to time. We are human, after all. If we learn from our mistakes, author John Maxwell says, then we pass the test of life and get promoted. If we do not learn from our mistakes, the lesson will be repeated, only next time it will be harder—suffering is a great teacher. Maxwell says that we know we have learned our lesson when our actions actually change.[1] Meanwhile, we should see our mistakes as lessons, not horrors, forgiving ourselves.

We need to seek forgiveness from God and from those we have harmed, too. Forgiveness is a key that will open the door to our souls' peace and rest. Jesus gave us this key: "Forgive us our sins, as we have forgiven those who sin against us," and "If you forgive those who sin against you, your heavenly Father will forgive you. But if you refuse to forgive others, your Father will not forgive your sins" (Matthew 6:12; 6:14–15 NLT).

Are you holding onto a grudge against someone? Sometimes we carry resentment in our hearts for years, soiling and limiting ourselves unconsciously. If you've made a mistake and need forgiveness, be sure to forgive others, too.

Prayer

Lord, I made a mistake. I missed Your clearly defined target for my life as stated in Your Holy Word. I gave in to human weakness. I feel badly about this. I want to stand before You without sin pulling me away from the closeness we usually enjoy. Please forgive me my mistake. I will do all I can not to repeat it. I know I need to forgive others if I am to be forgiven, so I release those who have sinned against me from my grudges and resentment. I am not the judge of others; You are, and You are merciful. I pray for those who have despitefully used me and I ask for Your forgiveness upon them and upon me. In Jesus' name I pray.

---

1 John Maxwell, *Failing Forward* (Nashville, TN: Thomas Nelson, 2000), 13.

Devotional Notes & Scripture References

_____

_____

_____

_____

_____

_____

_____

_____

_____

_____

_____

_____

_____

_____

_____

_____

_____

_____

_____

_____

_____

_____

_____

_____

_____

_____

Devotional Notes & Scripture References

_____

_____

_____

_____

_____

_____

_____

_____

_____

_____

_____

_____

_____

_____

_____

_____

_____

_____

_____

_____

_____

_____

_____

_____

DAY 5 - WHEN HELP IS
A LONG TIME COMING

Sometimes people believe that God does not answer prayers. His silence can be profound. Sometimes, too, He has answered our prayers, but we just didn't accept the answer!

The Well-Watered Life tells the story of Isaac and Rebecca's infertility. Desperate desire for a child can be like wandering in an endless desert, wondering where the oasis of conception could be. Women who cannot conceive are often called *barren*, as if their own bodies were a desert. Isaac was forty when he married Rebecca and did not father his twins until he was sixty. Twenty years of infertility! Yet Isaac did not lose faith in God's promise. He prayed until his prayers were answered.

Another example of long-term patience and faith is the woman whom Jesus healed of persistent bleeding. She'd had this problem for twelve long years. Yet this patient woman had so much faith she believed, "If I can just touch his robe, I will be healed." Jesus turned to look at her. He said, "'Daughter, be encouraged! Your faith has made you well.' And the woman was healed at that moment" (Matthew 9:20-22, NLT).

Twenty years. Twelve years. Some prayers take a long time to be answered, but we can always know that, even if it is a long time coming, help is on the way.

Prayer

Lord, I know some things take time, just as a mighty oak takes time to grow from a small acorn. I have faith that underneath it all, You are building me a root network; You are laying the groundwork for the support I will need; You are actively nourishing and nurturing the soil so as to perform the mighty work in my life that I have asked for and also in the lives of those I intercede for. Thank You that You listen and answer every prayer, all in good time. In Jesus' name I pray. Amen.

Devotional Notes & Scripture References

_____

_____

_____

_____

_____

_____

_____

_____

_____

_____

_____

_____

_____

_____

_____

_____

_____

_____

_____

_____

_____

_____

_____

_____

Devotional Notes & Scripture References

_____

_____

_____

_____

_____

_____

_____

_____

_____

_____

_____

_____

_____

_____

_____

_____

_____

_____

_____

_____

_____

_____

_____

_____

DAY 6 - THE RESULTS OF OBEDIENCE

The Well-Watered Life recounts how Isaac obeyed God even when it was inconvenient. In the midst of drought and famine, Isaac planned go to Egypt where there might be water and employment. However, God told him to go to Gerar, the land of the Philistines. Isaac obeyed and prospered greatly.

After returning from the Persian Gulf War, several of us soldiers were invited to share our testimonies of 'God's goodness to us while we were in Saudi Arabia. We shared how the Lord had preserved us through dangers, had allowed us to share our faith and bring other soldiers to faith in Christ. Then I felt led to share the last command my platoon sergeant had issued to me, which was to bury in the sand some Bibles written in Arabic and English as there was no way to transport them. I had obeyed that command. When I finished this story of burying Bibles in the desert sand, the pastor and the whole congregation began to weep, rejoice, and worship the Lord. They had been praying fervently for the Lord to plant His word in Saudi Arabia! I had done so—with obedience and a shovel!

Prayer

Lord, we do not see all ends, but You do. Help me to have more faith that You do not issue commands arbitrarily. Your commands are rooted in great wisdom and purpose, and they always bring benefit, even if we cannot see it at the time. Obedience is not always easy, but let us have faith that You will bring about great works when we follow Your commands. We can "rest" assured that if we obey You and do the planting, You will bring about the harvest. Let my life be given over to obedience to You, knowing that the fruits will always be good. In Jesus' name I pray.

Devotional Notes & Scripture References

_____

_____

_____

_____

_____

_____

_____

_____

_____

_____

_____

_____

_____

_____

_____

_____

_____

_____

_____

_____

_____

_____

_____

_____

_____

Devotional Notes & Scripture References

_____

_____

_____

_____

_____

_____

_____

_____

_____

_____

_____

_____

_____

_____

_____

_____

_____

_____

_____

_____

_____

_____

_____

_____

_____

_____

_____

_____

_____

_____

_____

DAY 7 - HE RESTED ON
THE SEVENTH DAY

On the seventh day, God rested after creating the world (Genesis 2:2 NLT). Given the abundance of species in nature—plus the creation of the towering mountains, deep oceans, stars, and planets—God needed a rest! He had performed a gargantuan and intricate work. After a work week, we are usually pretty tired too, and we want and need to rest.

The greatest way to refresh ourselves is by basking in the presence of the Lord. We can let our guards down over the weekend, when we're free from the pressures of the work week. We can go to the Lord early on an unhurried Saturday morning and have some quiet time with Him. The Lord has watched over us with loving eyes throughout the week, waiting anxiously for us to call out to Him in prayer. The Lord promised that if we seek Him, we will find Him (Matthew 7:7 NLT). He is there for us with the same attention to detail He gave to the universe—even the hairs on our heads have been numbered (Matthew 10:30 KJV). We are known, we are loved, and we are understood.

Resting is when we let go of all the stress and strain and get in tune with the most essential part of our human nature—the part that is meant to be one with Him. Then we will experience rest and peace.

Prayer

Lord, it has been another hectic week. You know how much energy and time go into all the work involved in life on this earth. Now that rest time has come I want to be with You, replenishing our relationship, tasting Your beautiful peace, and comprehending Your wisdom and guidance. I want to nourish my life in Your Spirit, where the most precious, important, and eternal things are so that I can be a blessing to all those around me—an instrument of Your love and peace. Thank You, Lord, for Your life-filled love.
In Jesus' name I pray.

Devotional Notes & Scripture References

_____

_____

_____

_____

_____

_____

_____

_____

_____

_____

_____

_____

_____

_____

_____

_____

_____

_____

_____

_____

_____

_____

_____

_____

_____

_____

Devotional Notes & Scripture References

_____

_____

_____

_____

_____

_____

_____

_____

_____

_____

_____

_____

_____

_____

_____

_____

_____

_____

_____

_____

_____

_____

_____

_____

DAY 8 - THE OVERLOAD SYNDROME

There is no doubt we live in stressful times. Thanks to the Information Age, we get all the bad news instantly and in living color. Our modern conveniences like smart phones sometimes add to our burdens. We're on overload: too much to do, too much information, and too much stress.

It may be comforting to know that people faced overload even in ancient times. Think about our friend Isaac. He not only suffered from a famine, he was ordered by God not to seek relief in Egypt but to go to Gerar. Questions like, "How will I support my family in Gerar?" must have bombarded 'Isaac's mind as he saw his wife and children growing thin with hunger.

Yet in Isaac's time of need, God appeared to him and reassured him about all His promises (Genesis 26:1-6 NLT). He will reassure us and unburden us too if we go to Him in prayer.

Prayer

Lord, sometimes the stresses of life are just overwhelming. Let me remember that You are always there to hear my prayers and heed all my concerns. I know You know all about me and my life; You know all the struggles of humanity, and You want to help and be a part of it all. It says in Revelation 3:20 (KJV): "Behold, I stand at the door and knock. If any man hears My voice and opens the door, I will come in to him and will sup with him and he with Me." I want to hear Your voice and open the door. I want to have a living relationship with You every day and experience the peace that passes understanding (Philippians 4:7 KJV). I know that You are greater than anything I face, and can remove any burden I carry, for you have said, "Come to me, all of you who are weary and carry heavy burdens, and I will give you rest" (Matthew 11:28 NLT). Relieve me from overload so I may better do Your will. In Jesus' name I pray. Amen.

Devotional Notes & Scripture References

_____

_____

_____

_____

_____

_____

_____

_____

_____

_____

_____

_____

_____

_____

_____

_____

_____

_____

_____

_____

_____

_____

_____

_____

_____

Devotional Notes & Scripture References

_____

_____

_____

_____

_____

_____

_____

_____

_____

_____

_____

_____

_____

_____

_____

_____

_____

_____

_____

_____

_____

_____

_____

_____

_____

_____

_____

DAY 9 - THE PURPOSE
OF THE COMFORTER

The Comforter is the Holy Spirit, sometimes called the Holy Ghost. The King James Version uses the word Comforter for the Greek word *paraclete*, but the New Living Translation translates this as our Advocate— the one who speaks to the Father in our defense. Other translations include encourager, counselor, helper, advisor, exhorter, strengthener, and intercessor. In the physical absence of Jesus, we relate with the Comforter or Advocate, as Jesus promised (John 14:16 KJV, NLT). In fact, Jesus assured us that the Comforter or Advocate was so desirable that the disciples should be happy Jesus was going away, because otherwise the Comforter couldn't come (John 16:17). Jesus presented the Comforter as an eternal companion (John 14:16) and teacher to remind us of all that Jesus said on earth (John 14:26). The Comforter is indispensable for our spiritual lives.

When the Lord appeared to Isaac to comfort him, we do not know what form He took, but He certainly consoled Isaac in his hour of doubt and need (Genesis 26:1-6, NLT). So we will be comforted in difficult times. Jesus promised us peace after he spoke of sending the Comforter: "Peace I leave with you; my peace I give you. I do not give to you as the world gives. Do not let your hearts be troubled and do not be afraid" (John 14: 27, New International Version). Our hearts are eased and cleansed; our burdens are lifted as the Lord answers our heartfelt petitions for forgiveness and guidance. The priceless gift of the Holy Spirit comes to us as rest for our hearts. Let's thank the Lord for this incomparable gift.

Prayer

Lord, Jesus left us peace and a Comforter. We are led into truth, knowledge, understanding, and forgiveness by the Holy Spirit. We bow down and honor the Comforter and beg for its indwelling in our hearts. We don't deserve this freely given gift, but let us meet this grace through faith and be cleansed, encouraged, taught, and made whole in You. Thank You for sending such a beautiful and priceless gift to humankind. Thank You, Lord, our strength and our redeemer. In Jesus' name I pray. Amen.

Devotional Notes & Scripture References

_____

_____

_____

_____

_____

_____

_____

_____

_____

_____

_____

_____

_____

_____

_____

_____

_____

_____

_____

_____

_____

_____

_____

_____

Devotional Notes & Scripture References

_____

_____

_____

_____

_____

_____

_____

_____

_____

_____

_____

_____

_____

_____

_____

_____

_____

_____

_____

_____

_____

_____

_____

_____

DAY 10 - THE DOVE
THAT COULDN'T REST ITS FEET

In *The Well-Watered Life*, we saw how Abraham's family was chosen for a great purpose. The Lord promised to bless all the nations of the earth through the descendants of Abraham, Isaac, and Jacob. Indeed, they were the forefathers of three of the world's great faiths: Judaism, Christianity, and Islam.

The flood story surrounding Noah's family also had great providential significance. The world had become so corrupt that God was deeply angered. He decided to wipe out the rest of humanity and start over with a man he could trust. Noah built an ark, and then the rains drowned everyone on earth except Noah's family.

It must have been a terrifying passage: thunder, lightning, and always having to bail the decks. There was nowhere to land or rest. The family had to wait until the great waters receded. They sent out a raven and then a dove to scout out land (Genesis 8:8 NLT).

In its first flight, the poor dove searched but found nowhere to rest its feet (Genesis 8:9 NLT). It must have been exhausted by the time it returned to the ark. The second time the dove flew out, it returned with a branch in its beak. Noah knew they were saved—dry land was near. The Holy Spirit is sometimes likened to a dove—and doesn't the Holy Spirit cover the earth, looking for a place to rest, looking for hearts in which to dwell, looking for people of faith?

Prayer

Lord, let Your Holy Spirit rest in my heart. Let my life, my thoughts, words, and actions be pleasing to You, and let me be one with Your will. I need the comfort, guidance, and grace of Your Holy Spirit every hour. I cannot steer my ark without You. Please help me to deal with the challenges of this day, knowing that if I faithfully follow You, I will find a safe shore after every storm. In Jesus' name I pray. Amen.

Devotional Notes & Scripture References

_____

_____

_____

_____

_____

_____

_____

_____

_____

_____

_____

_____

_____

_____

_____

_____

_____

_____

_____

_____

_____

_____

_____

_____

Devotional Notes & Scripture References

_____

_____

_____

_____

_____

_____

_____

_____

_____

_____

_____

_____

_____

_____

_____

_____

_____

_____

_____

_____

_____

_____

_____

DAY 11 - THE COMMAND TO REST

As we frantically try to achieve more and more in our lives, we sometimes forget to rest. Yet in those moments, the Lord speaks to us in special ways. The Lord appeared to Isaac at night (Genesis 26:24, NLT), a time of rest, to reaffirm His covenant with him. He appeared to Isaac's son, Jacob, in a dream (Genesis 28:10-15, NLT).

We are commanded by God to rest on the Sabbath. Exodus 16:23, NLT says, "This is what the Lord commanded: Tomorrow will be a day of complete rest, a holy Sabbath day set apart for the Lord." In the Ten Commandments (Exodus 20: 8–11), He said: "Remember to observe the Sabbath day by keeping it holy. You have six days each week for your ordinary work, but the seventh day is a Sabbath day of rest dedicated to the Lord your God...For in six days the Lord made the heavens, the earth, the sea, and everything in them; but on the seventh day he rested."

This is repeated in Exodus 23:12 and Exodus 31:15, NLT. This is practical: rest restores our energies for our work; it is also spiritual, for in times of rest, God can steal into our hearts and speak in special ways.

Prayer

Lord, there is so much work to do, six days a week hardly seems enough. Yet I know that it is in the resting times, the quiet times, the times of holy music, fellowship, and solitude that You are able to speak to my calmed heart. Let me set aside time for You each morning and evening—the quiet or restful times of the day—and remember the Sabbath and keep it holy so that You may speak to me to change my life and make it more directed toward You. Thank You. In Jesus' name I pray. Amen.

Devotional Notes & Scripture References

_____

_____

_____

_____

_____

_____

_____

_____

_____

_____

_____

_____

_____

_____

_____

_____

_____

_____

_____

_____

_____

_____

_____

_____

Devotional Notes & Scripture References

_____

_____

_____

_____

_____

_____

_____

_____

_____

_____

_____

_____

_____

_____

_____

_____

_____

_____

_____

_____

_____

_____

_____

_____

_____

DAY 12 - RESTING THROUGH WORSHIP AND FELLOWSHIP

We are commanded to rest on the Sabbath and keep it holy (Exodus 16:23; 20:8–11; 23:12, and 31:15, NLT). This means worshipping God with fellow believers on your day of rest.

Sometimes going to church may not seem like rest. We must get up and be ready on time. We may worry about how we look. We may not like the preacher's message. Maybe that choir member was rude or arrogant, and we thought, "She isn't in Christ. Why is she up there?"

Yet the more we focus on worshipping God and treating our fellow worshippers with His love, the richer our church experience will be. It is an indispensable part of our spiritual lives, laying the foundation for a fruitful week. A phrase of a song may speak to us, a quote from the Bible may suddenly jump off the page, or a kind look or remark from a fellow worshipper may make our hearts glow. We need the grace and support of going to His house to raise our voices in prayer and praise with our fellow believers.

Going to church is like drinking at an inexhaustible fountain of the purest, most abundant waters. We should not ignore or bypass this important source of sustenance.

Prayer

Lord, going to church is sometimes burdensome, yet I always get something precious out of it. Brothers and sisters in Christ are the most beautiful and sincere people I know. I need their fellowship and the strengthening of church attendance. I need the beauty of the music and the flowers. I need to give You my heart and attention completely, at least for those few hours per week. Thank You that in this land there is freedom of worship and a church on every block. Thank You that people have answered the call to ministry. Thank You that I have money for the collection basket. I pray that You will give us a passion to be a witness to our neighbors who are lost and also need you. In Jesus' name I pray. Amen.

Devotional Notes & Scripture References

_____

_____

_____

_____

_____

_____

_____

_____

_____

_____

_____

_____

_____

_____

_____

_____

_____

_____

_____

_____

_____

_____

_____

_____

_____

_____

_____

Devotional Notes & Scripture References

_____

_____

_____

_____

_____

_____

_____

_____

_____

_____

_____

_____

_____

_____

_____

_____

_____

_____

_____

_____

_____

_____

_____

_____

_____

_____

DAY 13 - THE POWER OF REST

Resting may not seem powerful; it may seem passive, weak, or even lazy. Yet resting is potent if it means we get out of the way of the most powerful Being in the universe. It is powerful if we say: "Thy will, not mine, be done." We then surrender our will to His, laying down our defenses and admitting humbly that the power, the glory, and the results are in His hands. We aren't the lords of the universe—He is.

Surrendering to God does not mean giving up; just giving up our egos. We aren't turning things over to chance; we are presenting the case formally to Him in prayer in full recognition of His power, His wisdom, and His better judgment. It means coming boldly before the throne of grace with faith: "Because of Christ and our faith in him, we can now come boldly and confidently into God's presence" (Ephesians 3:12 NLT).

This is rest. This is moving our egos, our desires, and our compulsive needs for control out of His way so He can work. This is sweet surrender to the One who always knows best: Our Father who art in heaven (Matthew 6:9 KJV).

Prayer

Lord, help me to surrender utterly to You. This does not mean I have no responsibility; it means that I live within Your will and pray that Your will be done in all situations. The Bible says, "Those who live in the shelter of the Most High will find rest in the shadow of the Almighty" (Psalm 91:1 NLT). It means my humble obedience and quiet submission, my sweet surrender to let You have Your own way, Lord. Your ways and wisdom are always best. I give over to You all my concerns, all my pride, all my faith in my own abilities to do and solve things. You are the molder of men and the mover of events, not me. I rest in You, Lord. Thy will be done. In Jesus' name I pray. Amen.

Devotional Notes & Scripture References

_____

_____

_____

_____

_____

_____

_____

_____

_____

_____

_____

_____

_____

_____

_____

_____

_____

_____

_____

_____

_____

_____

_____

_____

_____

Devotional Notes & Scripture References

_____

_____

_____

_____

_____

_____

_____

_____

_____

_____

_____

_____

_____

_____

_____

_____

_____

_____

_____

_____

_____

_____

_____

_____

DAY 14 - RESTING THROUGH CULTIVATING BETTER RELATIONSHIPS

Relationships can be sources of joy and support; they can also be sources of strife and pain. Sometimes the same relationship is a source of both happiness and pain.

There is only one way to deal with the ups and downs of earthly relationships: staying deep within the relationship that really counts: our relationship with God. No person is perfect. No one will fulfill all our needs. Only the Lord can do this. The Lord is the one constant companion, the one who completely understands, the one who has the love, grace, and wisdom for any situation we face. And the more we exercise His virtues in our relationships, the more beautiful those relationships will be.

God gives us the instruction to forgive others. When we forgive others our own hearts experience peace, and the pain is eased. Resigning from our self-appointed position as judge of others brings relief and rest in His bosom of grace.

Prayer

Lord, I am often at least partly at fault when my relationships go awry, and I need Your forgiveness. We are instructed to forgive others if we want to be forgiven (Matthew 6:14-15 KJV), so let me be forgiving of my fellow human beings who fall short of Your glory just as I do. We also know that we are blessed when others speak against us when we are not at fault (Matthew 5:11-12), so let me turn to You when someone has hurt me. You alone understand both that person and me; You alone love us enough to permeate with grace our relationships with our spouses, children, parents, friends, and neighbors. You alone are the seat of understanding, yet You do not judge us when we do not judge others (Luke: 6:37 KJV). Let me put You first in my life; I know then that all other relationships will fall into place. In Jesus' name I pray.

Devotional Notes & Scripture References

_____

_____

_____

_____

_____

_____

_____

_____

_____

_____

_____

_____

_____

_____

_____

_____

_____

_____

_____

_____

_____

_____

_____

_____

_____

Devotional Notes & Scripture References

_____

_____

_____

_____

_____

_____

_____

_____

_____

_____

_____

_____

_____

_____

_____

_____

_____

_____

_____

_____

_____

_____

_____

_____

DAY 15 - RESTING THROUGH BETTER STEWARDSHIP

In *The Well-Watered Life*, it was noted that some Americans are jealous of foreign immigrants who succeed in buying homes, accumulating wealth, and raising kids who go to the best colleges without the parents even being able to speak English.

When people prosper like this, there is blessing behind it, we may be sure. These people use their God-given talents and are virtuous in ways that please the Lord.

Isaac prospered in a foreign land too. Escaping famine and the equivalent of a desert depression, he wanted to go to the greener fields of Egypt, but the Lord ordered him into Gerar, where he was a total foreigner. Obediently, Isaac went, and by the time he left he was a wealthy man. He used what he had in the best way he could. Isaac "acquired so many flocks of sheep and goats, herds of cattle, and servants that the Philistines became jealous of him" (Genesis 26:14 NLT). He was a good steward of the Lord's gifts to him, working with what he had, and the Lord blessed him accordingly.

Prayer

Lord, I know that You have promised that we would have life and have it more abundantly (John 10:10 KJV). Thank You for all that I have been given: the internal gifts, the support, help, advice of elders, schooling, free libraries, and opportunities in an abundant land. I want to grow in gratitude for all that I have rather than thinking about what more I would like. Let me make the most of my God-given gifts in order to prosper in this world, contribute to Your church, and help my family. Let me apply my talents with integrity, developing them diligently, knowing that as I do so You will bless me with all I need. In Jesus' name I pray. Amen.

Devotional Notes & Scripture References

_____

_____

_____

_____

_____

_____

_____

_____

_____

_____

_____

_____

_____

_____

_____

_____

_____

_____

_____

_____

_____

_____

_____

_____

Devotional Notes & Scripture References

_____

_____

_____

_____

_____

_____

_____

_____

_____

_____

_____

_____

_____

_____

_____

_____

_____

_____

_____

_____

_____

_____

_____

_____

DAY 16 - REST COMES FROM BECOMING AN EFFECTIVE LEADER

You may or may not be a leader at your place of employment. Yet if you are a parent, you are a leader to your children. You are also the leader of your own life. You are in charge of your choices. A good leader finds rest through wise decision-making.

A person feels restful after making a good judgment call both in the moment and in the long run as he or she grows in confidence to handle things well.

Isaac was a leader. He not only led his family, he was treated as a leader in a foreign land. In Genesis 26, Abimelech (the king) came to ask Isaac for peace (rest) as if Isaac were on the same level as a king. Why? Because Abimelech saw that God was with Isaac. "We can plainly see that the Lord is with you," (Genesis 26:28 NLT) he told Isaac.

When the Lord is with you and in you, people can sense it. They instinctively turn to you for leadership. How do we make sure the Lord is with us and in us? We turn to the One who said, "Believe that I am in the Father and the Father is in me" (John 14:11 NLT).

Prayer

Lord, You are the leader of all. Yet I am the leader of my own life and should set an example and lead others wherever I go because, as a believer, I represent You. Let me order my life so that I am in the Spirit; I am partaking of Your love, Your light, and Your guidance so I may make rightful decisions with a wisdom beyond my own. Help me to stay within Your will and Your Word so that I have good words, advice, and Your love to give to others. Let me make wise decisions I would not have made without Your Spirit leading me; clarifying my vision, and speaking to my heart. In Jesus' name I pray.

Devotional Notes & Scripture References

_____

_____

_____

_____

_____

_____

_____

_____

_____

_____

_____

_____

_____

_____

_____

_____

_____

_____

_____

_____

_____

_____

_____

_____

_____

_____

_____

_____

Devotional Notes & Scripture References

_____

_____

_____

_____

_____

_____

_____

_____

_____

_____

_____

_____

_____

_____

_____

_____

_____

_____

_____

_____

_____

_____

_____

DAY 17 - BE FILLED DAILY WITH THE HOLY SPIRIT

As was said in the last section, we can rest in our good leadership and decision-making if we are in Christ. We stay in Christ through daily (not weekly) worship, study of the Word, and prayer. We need fresh infusions of the Holy Spirit on a daily basis, because the world and Satan do everything they can to wear us down and out; to get us to make costly and painful mistakes. We need strengthening of our inner selves so that we can withstand the onslaught of evil.

Reading the Word rids our minds of the debris of the world. The Word speaks of eternal things of the Spirit. Worship—giving praise and thanks—communicates with God such that the Spirit can flow into us and fill us with strength and peace. In prayer, we can make our requests known to God and rest assured that He hears and answers. "…in every thing by prayer and supplication with thanksgiving let your requests be made known unto God. And the peace of God, which passeth all understanding, shall keep your hearts and minds through Christ Jesus" (Philippians 4:6-7, KJV).

Prayer

Lord, I am not strong enough to withstand the onslaught of evil from within and without me. I cannot control my temper or my words or habits without strength from You. Please strengthen me for the daily fight to live in a way that is pleasing to You. Let me enjoy the peace, rest, and joy of being filled with the Holy Spirit every day. This is the living water I cannot do without. There is no substitute for it; there are only cheap imitations. I need and want the Holy Spirit to live with me and in me, and I ask for this gift this day. In Jesus' name I pray.

Devotional Notes & Scripture References

_____

_____

_____

_____

_____

_____

_____

_____

_____

_____

_____

_____

_____

_____

_____

_____

_____

_____

_____

_____

_____

_____

_____

_____

Devotional Notes & Scripture References

_____

_____

_____

_____

_____

_____

_____

_____

_____

_____

_____

_____

_____

_____

_____

_____

_____

_____

_____

_____

_____

_____

_____

_____

_____

DAY 18 - RESTING IN THE MIDST OF ADVERSITY

We all have trials. The great people of faith in the Bible had them too, so we can hardly hope to escape all adversity. As was depicted in *The Well-Watered Life*, Isaac of old went through at least nine crises in his life and came out the victor in all of them. He had faith, he (mostly) displayed good character, and he was obedient to the Lord's commands even when things didn't look so good and were, in fact, dangerous to his and to his whole family's well-being (Genesis 25, 26 NLT).

Crisis is the time to have faith and rest in the Lord. Jesus demonstrated this when he was out in a boat with his disciples (Matthew 24–27 NLT): "Suddenly, a fierce storm struck the lake, with waves breaking into the boat. But Jesus was sleeping. The disciples went and woke him up, shouting, 'Lord, save us! We're going to drown!' Jesus responded, 'Why are you afraid? You have so little faith!' Then he got up and rebuked the wind and waves, and suddenly there was a great calm. The disciples were amazed. 'Who is this man?' they asked. 'Even the winds and waves obey him!'"

Prayer

Lord, You know the depth and breadth of the adversity I am facing. You know the exact measurements of the crisis. You know how frightened I am in this storm and how afraid I am of the utter shipwreck of all my dreams and plans and how concerned I am for my family. I ask You to pass Your hand over this crisis and still the winds and waters. If even the winds and waves obeyed You in ancient times, I know that You are the master over this storm in my life too. Grant me peace and rest in the knowledge that You are at the helm of my little boat and You will see me safely to shore. Nothing is beyond Your great power if I only have faith in You. In Jesus' name I pray.

Devotional Notes & Scripture References

_____
_____
_____
_____
_____
_____
_____
_____
_____
_____
_____
_____
_____
_____
_____
_____
_____
_____
_____
_____
_____
_____
_____
_____
_____

Devotional Notes & Scripture References

_____

_____

_____

_____

_____

_____

_____

_____

_____

_____

_____

_____

_____

_____

_____

_____

_____

_____

_____

_____

_____

_____

_____

_____

_____

_____

DAY 19 - SOMETIMES YOU HAVE TO WAR IN THE SPIRIT BEFORE YOUR REST COMES

Sometimes finding or making the time to rest is a wrestling match with our schedules! Sometimes, too, when we have finally carved out some space, we feel depressed and confused facing unstructured time. Psychologists have found that many Americans suffer from depression on Sunday afternoons, because it is a time when they may have a few hours with nothing to do. We're lost when we have leisure time!

This is the time to offer our rest time to God. Satan is seeking to wear out believers; to discourage them and tire them out, the way a heavyweight champion may seek to tire out his opponent or a winning team might try to run out the clock. When we're weary and worn-out, used up and lacking refreshment we are vulnerable to attack by the evil one. Our defenses and resistance are low. We are beaten down, ready to respond to a crisis by lashing out at our loved ones or by doing something unhealthy for a temporary high. We have to give ourselves permission to rest for the sake of the greater causes we serve, and we seek this permission from the Lord.

Prayer

Lord, I am taking some rest now. I don't want to feel guilty over a little time in front of the TV, or going shopping, or stopping for a frozen yogurt because I have worked very hard. If I don't give myself a break, I will be weak in the face of temptations. I want to stay strong in my many responsibilities; I want to be accountable and ready with a loving heart when my family and friends call upon me. I am not being selfish by seeking refreshment; I am trying to refill my reservoirs so I can keep going in the desert of this world. Thank You for this time of refreshment and rest. I pray it can make me more effective, truer, more loving, and more giving. In Jesus' name I pray.

Devotional Notes & Scripture References

_____

_____

_____

_____

_____

_____

_____

_____

_____

_____

_____

_____

_____

_____

_____

_____

_____

_____

_____

_____

_____

_____

_____

Devotional Notes & Scripture References

_____

_____

_____

_____

_____

_____

_____

_____

_____

_____

_____

_____

_____

_____

_____

_____

_____

_____

_____

_____

_____

_____

_____

_____

_____

_____

DAY 20 - DROPPING YOUR NET TO FOLLOW CHRIST

When Jesus called the Apostles, they literally dropped what they were doing and followed. Matthew (4:18–20 NLT) tells us: "One day as Jesus was walking along the shore of the Sea of Galilee, he saw two brothers—Simon, also called Peter, and Andrew—throwing a net into the water, for they fished for a living. Jesus called out to them, 'Come, follow me, and I will show you how to fish for people!' And they left their nets at once and followed him."

In the Old Testament of the Holy Bible, Isaac continually picked up his tents and went where the Lord told him, even to a foreign land; even away from seeming prosperity.

There are times too, when we must drop everything we are doing—drop our nets—and follow him. Leave the workplace behind and all the concerns of daily life—the bills and the mortgage and the kids' school. Just drop that net and follow Him. Let go and let God. If we bring it all to Him, it will be taken care of.

Prayer

Lord, sometimes it is all too much for me to sort out. Human error, emotions, ego, and the devil all get in the way and seem to form a snare I am caught up in, and I cannot cut or fight my way out of it unless I turn it over to You. I believe that if I seek Your will in all I do, You will show which path to take (Proverbs 3:6 NLT). I know that it is not by force nor by strength, but by Your Spirit that all battles are won (Zechariah 4:6 NLT). If there are times when You literally need me to change my job, change my locale, and change my life I pray that I can hear and heed Your guidance. When You call, let my answer be, "Yes, Lord." Let me stop what I am doing, drop my net, and say, "I am coming, Lord." In Jesus' name I pray.

Devotional Notes & Scripture References

_____

_____

_____

_____

_____

_____

_____

_____

_____

_____

_____

_____

_____

_____

_____

_____

_____

_____

_____

_____

_____

_____

_____

_____

Devotional Notes & Scripture References

_____

_____

_____

_____

_____

_____

_____

_____

_____

_____

_____

_____

_____

_____

_____

_____

_____

_____

_____

_____

_____

_____

_____

_____

_____

DAY 21- EVERYONE WANTS REST

Many people seek recreation, thinking it will give them rest. There is nothing wrong with recreation, but if it becomes a frantic pursuit we will probably find ourselves dissatisfied all over again. The only true rest and peace is in the Lord.

Jesus said, "Come to me, all of you who are weary and carry heavy burdens, and I will give you rest" (Matthew 11:28, NLT). He also tells us to come before the altar and make our petitions known and be filled with "the peace of God, which passeth all understanding" (Philippians 4:7 KJV). That peace is the greatest rest for our souls. It is what we all seek, even when we use substitutes like alcohol and other drugs, pornography, affairs, all-night partying and carrying on. What we really want is rest and respite for our souls, and there's only one place to get it.

"Rest in the Lord," King David tells us (Psalm 37:7 KJV) and wait patiently for Him. "Fret not," he says, (Psalm 37:1 KJV) for "the meek shall inherit the earth; and shall delight themselves in the abundance of peace" (Psalm 37:11 KJV).

Rest and peace for the soul come from God. He is our satisfying portion.

Prayer

Lord, in our frenetic, stressful days and lives we are often restless. St. Augustine said our hearts would always be restless until we found our rest in You. When I seek comfort, peace, well-being, love, and satisfaction let me seek it from You rather than from the world or from other people or from things. Let me act in the knowledge that there is a well of living water, the kind which if I drink it, I will never thirst again (John 4:13 NLT). When I am tired, lonely, angry, hurt, upset, frantic, and stressed let me turn to You as the source of the rest and peace my soul craves. In Jesus' name I pray. Amen.

Devotional Notes & Scripture References

_____

_____

_____

_____

_____

_____

_____

_____

_____

_____

_____

_____

_____

_____

_____

_____

_____

_____

_____

_____

_____

_____

_____

_____

_____

_____

_____

_____

Devotional Notes & Scripture References

_____

_____

_____

_____

_____

_____

_____

_____

_____

_____

_____

_____

_____

_____

_____

_____

_____

_____

_____

_____

_____

_____

_____

_____

_____

_____

_____

_____

DAY 22 - FREEDOM FROM PERFORMING

"Let your hair down."

"Let it all hang out."

These expressions from the 1960s indicated a time when you could be free from performing and just be yourself. The advice to "be yourself" is all around us, yet that is often the hardest thing to do. Do we really even know ourselves? Aren't there layers of denial, pretense, approval-seeking, hidden resentments, fear, et cetera between us and our true selves?

Isaac, our model figure of faith, once denied who he was, saying he was Rebecca's brother, not her husband, in order to save his own skin. What a relief it must have been for him to stop lying and come clean as a man of God!

We should not try to cover up who we are. Our core identity is as children of God conformed to the image of His son (Romans 8:15, 29 NLT). That's enough! We don't have to measure up to anything else. We need to polish that image with study, prayer, and, most of all, repentance. When we repent, we throw away the image we have so carefully cultivated in front of others. We discard our desire to outperform others with our breakneck competitiveness. We bring it all to His altar and ask for mercy. We may shed tears at such a sincere time, but that's all right. Our Father understands.

Prayer

Lord, St. Paul told us to call upon you as our own *Abba* or *Papa* (Romans 8:15 NKJV). You are Lord of heaven and earth, but you are our Daddy too, loving us with a father's love. Let me find my identity, my core self in You. Let me strive to reflect Your image, not for the world's praise. All I want, forever, is to rest in Your heart as Your child, Your man or woman, Your own. In Jesus' name I pray.

Devotional Notes & Scripture References

_____

_____

_____

_____

_____

_____

_____

_____

_____

_____

_____

_____

_____

_____

_____

_____

_____

_____

_____

_____

_____

_____

_____

_____

_____

_____

_____

Devotional Notes & Scripture References

_____

_____

_____

_____

_____

_____

_____

_____

_____

_____

_____

_____

_____

_____

_____

_____

_____

_____

_____

_____

_____

_____

_____

_____

DAY 23 - UNPLUG DAILY TO REST

Have you ever noticed that when the electricity, your cell phone, your computer, or TV is on the fritz, there is an element of peace and rest? Sometimes our modern labor-saving devices take away from our rest

You can literally or symbolically unplug all your devices for a time each morning and evening to be with the Lord and start paying attention to your soul. Make some time each day to "steal away to Jesus." Early morning is a wonderful time—before the world awakens, before people feel they have a right to call you, before your work begins. Evening can provide a quiet segment of time as well when you can go and hide under the shelter of His wings. King David knew this, in his stress-filled, fugitive life: "All humanity finds shelter in the shadow of your wings" (Psalm 36:7 NLT). In fact, finding shelter and respite under God's wings was a theme of this great king of Israel. In Psalm 61:4 (NLT), he begged, "Let me live forever in your sanctuary, safe beneath the shelter of your wings!" What was more, because of God's great grace and aid, going into the shelter of God was ecstasy to David: "Because you are my helper, I sing for joy in the shadow of your wings" (Psalm 63:7 NLT). It can be our ecstasy too, every day.

Prayer

Lord, I want to make time each day to steal away to Jesus and the shelter of Your wings. Show me and help me find and take advantage of pockets of time when I can leave the world behind and nestle under Your wings and be protected. Help me have the courage to unplug this noisy, demanding, fast-paced world of ours and find some rest in You. I know You appeared and spoke to Isaac and Jacob of old during times of rest. Please speak to me when I am resting from the world in You. In Jesus' name I pray.

Devotional Notes & Scripture References

_____

_____

_____

_____

_____

_____

_____

_____

_____

_____

_____

_____

_____

_____

_____

_____

_____

_____

_____

_____

_____

_____

_____

Devotional Notes & Scripture References

DAY 24 - "IT IS FINISHED!"
FINISHING WHAT GOD HAS COMMANDED TO RECEIVE HIS REST

There is no rest quite as satisfying as that taken after a job well done. A day when we gave our best, a day when we were productive at work and also invested significantly in relationships, and a day when we have our due refreshments and a bit of recreation is a day well spent. After such a day, our heads fall onto our pillows with a sigh of satisfaction. The rest we take is more delicious than after days when we fell short; days when we couldn't forgive and are kept awake by resentment and adrenaline; days when we didn't do our best and knew it; days when we missed the chance to talk to our teenager because we were too busy watching the game or preparing dinner or surfing the Internet. When we finish our duties and responsibilities well and when day is done offer them to God, we receive due rest and peace. If we have fallen short—which we so often do—we must repent and plan to do better tomorrow. As long as He sees us trying—working and striving to be the kind of people He wants us to be— He will grant us rest.

Prayer

Lord, I wasn't all that I could have been today, but I gave my best effort. I am grateful I could feel genuine forgiveness in my heart when others fell short; I seek Your forgiveness for the times I fell short too. It was a fulfilling day. I enjoyed getting my work done, the foods I ate, the conversations I had, and the beauty of Your world. Now I lay down to sleep with my precious loved ones nearby, each cherished in his or her own way. Thank You for the restful darkness that soothes our eyes and minds to sleep. I look forward to another day of life tomorrow, and I thank You for this day of life today. Each and every day, and life itself, is a great gift. Day is done today. In Jesus' name I pray.

Devotional Notes & Scripture References

_____

_____

_____

_____

_____

_____

_____

_____

_____

_____

_____

_____

_____

_____

_____

_____

_____

_____

_____

_____

_____

_____

_____

_____

Devotional Notes & Scripture References

_____

_____

_____

_____

_____

_____

_____

_____

_____

_____

_____

_____

_____

_____

_____

_____

_____

_____

_____

_____

_____

_____

_____

_____

DAY 25 - TRIBULATION WITH REST

There are certainly times of tempest in our lives. Yet if we have built our house for the Lord, we can keep calm. How do we think Isaac felt when, in spite of his faith and his accommodating ways, the jealous Philistines chased him out of Gerar and disputed over and over any wells Isaac found? Isaac needed wells to sustain the life of his family and his herds. Yet Isaac calmly kept relocating, resting in his faith in the Lord until even his enemies, led by King Abimelech, asked him to make peace with them: "We can plainly see that the Lord is with you" (Genesis 26:28 NLT).

God promises us safety and protection if we stay within His will: "Trust in the Lord with all your heart; do not depend on your own understanding" (Proverbs 3:5 NLT). Ezekiel 28:26 says: "And they shall dwell safely therein, and shall build houses, and plant vineyards; yea, they shall dwell with confidence" (KJV).

Prayer

Lord, You know that my house is threatened by storm and flood. You know that there are adverse winds blowing and howling around me and mine. It is all too easy to let my heart grow tight and small with fear; to be faithless toward You and stop praying and giving in bitterness that these storms have come upon us. I don't want to be like that, Lord. I know You help us in thousands of ways each day; I know that there are reasons for these storms beyond my comprehension. I also know that You are a very present help in trouble. All I pray for is to live more closely within Your will; to be honest about the ways in which I am not, and to gain the strength to correct that. I have tried to build my house upon You, Lord, and I believe we will dwell in safety, peace, and plenty once this storm has blown over. In Jesus' name I pray.

Devotional Notes & Scripture References

_____

_____

_____

_____

_____

_____

_____

_____

_____

_____

_____

_____

_____

_____

_____

_____

_____

_____

_____

_____

_____

_____

_____

_____

Devotional Notes & Scripture References

_____

_____

_____

_____

_____

_____

_____

_____

_____

_____

_____

_____

_____

_____

_____

_____

_____

_____

_____

_____

_____

_____

_____

_____

DAY 26 - MAKE YOUR HOME A HOUSE OF REST

The Bible says, "When the enemy shall come in like a flood, the Spirit of the Lord shall lift up a standard against him" (Isaiah 59:19 KJV). Do we have the flag of God flying on our home? What is that standard? It is prayer, worship, and study.

Who does not want a house of peace? We all know: "Better a dry crust eaten in peace than a house filled with feasting—and conflict" (Proverbs 17:1 NLT). We all want to live in a home of peace, mutual support, and love. Hebrews 3:6 (NLT) advises us that "we are God's house, if we keep our courage and remain confident in our hope in Christ."

The Lord says in Revelation 3:20 (KJV): "Behold, I stand at the door and knock. If any man hears my voice and opens the door, I will come in to him and will sup with him and he with me." This passage indicates that God wants to live with us, to be with us on a daily, even an hourly, basis. He wants to be among us in our families, for wherever two or more are gathered in his name, there he will be also: "For where two or three are gathered together in my name, there am I in the midst of them" (Matthew 18:20 KJV).

Gather in his name as a family as often as you can. If family members won't join in, do it alone. The more you bring God into your home, the more peaceful, lovely, and happy it will be.

Prayer

Lord, thank You for the great gifts of the Bible, worship, faith, song, and prayer. Everyone wants a peaceful, happy home. I know that is impossible without Your presence. Lord, I want my house to be a place of rest with the sweet scent of Your presence and the beauty and joyfulness of prayer and song in the air. I invite You to dwell with us and between us, Lord, in our relationships and home. In Jesus' name I pray.

Devotional Notes & Scripture References

_____

_____

_____

_____

_____

_____

_____

_____

_____

_____

_____

_____

_____

_____

_____

_____

_____

_____

_____

_____

_____

_____

_____

_____

Devotional Notes & Scripture References

_____

_____

_____

_____

_____

_____

_____

_____

_____

_____

_____

_____

_____

_____

_____

_____

_____

_____

_____

_____

_____

_____

_____

_____

DAY 27 - SURRENDERING TO GOD'S REST BY FAITH DURING TIMES OF UNCERTAINTY

We all face times of uncertainty: financial, marital, career, legal issues, our children's problems, and anxiety about medical diagnoses. How can we rest during anxious times? There is only one way: put the outcome into the hands of the Lord.

As St. Paul said, "Faith…gives us assurance about things we cannot see. Through their faith, the people in days of old earned a good reputation" (Hebrews 11:1-2 NLT). Certainly Isaac was someone who put his faith in the Lord in times of uncertainty and anxiety. Likewise, the future king, David, lived in constant danger. Yet David gave us the most heartening verse for the anxiety of uncertainty that the world has ever known: "Yea, though I walk through the valley of the shadow of death, I will fear no evil: for thou art with me; thy rod and thy staff they comfort me. Thou preparest a table before me in the presence of mine enemies" (Psalm 23: 4-5 KJV). This literally happened to Isaac when he was exiled to the hostile valley of Gerar and finally Abimelech came to him and had a feast with him, allowing Isaac to enjoy a table with his enemies.

We are assured in Hebrews 13:5 (NLT): "For He Himself has said, "I will never leave you nor forsake you," and John 16:33 (NLT): "I have told you all this so that you may have peace in me. Here on earth you will have many trials and sorrows. But take heart, because I have overcome the world."

Prayer

Lord, human beings cannot see the future or the outcomes of all things. You know far more than I do about what is coming down the road. I cannot tell if it will be a desirable outcome, but I do know that You can work in all circumstances, and that even if things do not go well in this world of the flesh, if I am right with You, things will go well in the world of the spirit. Therefore, even if I am walking through the valley of the shadow of death I will not be anxious, for You are with me. In Jesus' name I pray.

Devotional Notes & Scripture References

_____

_____

_____

_____

_____

_____

_____

_____

_____

_____

_____

_____

_____

_____

_____

_____

_____

_____

_____

_____

_____

_____

_____

_____

Devotional Notes & Scripture References

_____

_____

_____

_____

_____

_____

_____

_____

_____

_____

_____

_____

_____

_____

_____

_____

_____

_____

_____

_____

_____

_____

_____

_____

_____

DAY 28 – REST BY CHOOSING TO FORGIVING OTHERS

Relationships are not always easy. Even among our most beloved family members and friends old and new conflicts may arise; feelings may be hurt, trust may be broken. Yet relationships are deeply fulfilling as well. We are meant to be together, not apart.

The Bible urges us to fellowship. Hebrews 10:25 (NLT) says: "Let us not neglect our meeting together, as some people do, but encourage one another." 1 John 1:7 (NLT) asserts that believers have fellowship. John 13:34 (NLT) tells us of Jesus' commandment: "Love each other. Just as I have loved you, you should love each other."

How can we love people who have hurt and offended us? We must forgive. Isaac is an example of forgiveness. Isaac was so forgiving that even though Esau married women who were "a grief of mind" to him and Rebecca (Genesis 26:35, New King James Version) Isaac still wanted to give Esau all he had. Our Lord Jesus Christ, of course, is the ultimate example of forgiveness. 1 John 2:11 enjoins us not to let the darkness of unforgiveness blind our eyes. We must forgive to live in restful relationships with others.

Prayer

Lord, I have been hurt by people and I know I have hurt others too. I admit to having hard feelings in my heart toward some people. Forgiving is not easy. Yet I know I must forgive in order to be forgiven; I know that if I do not show mercy, I will not be shown mercy. Also, if I truly understood the person's situation, I know my heart would melt with compassion and love You feel for him or her. Please give me more love in my heart toward my brethren, and let me forgive others their trespasses so You will forgive me mine. I want to rest in the joy and peace of good relationships with others. In Jesus' name I pray.

Devotional Notes & Scripture References

_____

_____

_____

_____

_____

_____

_____

_____

_____

_____

_____

_____

_____

_____

_____

_____

_____

_____

_____

_____

_____

_____

_____

_____

Devotional Notes & Scripture References

_____

_____

_____

_____

_____

_____

_____

_____

_____

_____

_____

_____

_____

_____

_____

_____

_____

_____

_____

_____

_____

_____

_____

_____

_____

_____

_____

_____

_____

DAY 29 - RESTING BY REJECTING THE WORLD'S IDOLS

We've spoken of unplugging ourselves from the various communications media of today in order to find rest. It is also important that we transcend the messages of the media for we cannot always escape them. It is hard to watch television any evening without encountering anti-Christian values. This is especially true of sexual messages. In the media, sexuality has been held up as an idol. The message that sex outside of marriage is normal is on almost every show.

1 John 2:16 (KJV) tells us: "For all that is in the world, the lust of the flesh, and the lust of the eyes and the pride of life is not of the Father," and Psalm 24:3-5 (NLT) enjoins us to have clean hands and pure hearts, not to worship idols of any kind and not to tell lies. In navigating this fallen world, we must not be naïve but be wise as serpents and innocent as doves (Matthew 10:16 KJV). This includes becoming media savvy and teaching our children to be so as well in order to give our souls rest from worldly idols.

Prayer

Lord, we are surrounded by media messages and content that are contrary to Your ways. Every movie, every TV show seems to hold up the idol of the human body and sexuality. Lord, let us have clean hands, pure minds, and willing hearts to turn away from these messages and this content and to point out every time we can to the young and to one another that these messages are harmful and untruthful and not in accordance with Your will and ways. Let us reaffirm the beauty of sexuality only within the sanctity of marriage. Let us refute any messages counter to this in our words, in our actions, and in our thoughts. In Jesus' name I pray.

Devotional Notes & Scripture References

_____

_____

_____

_____

_____

_____

_____

_____

_____

_____

_____

_____

_____

_____

_____

_____

_____

_____

_____

_____

_____

_____

Devotional Notes & Scripture References

_____

_____

_____

_____

_____

_____

_____

_____

_____

_____

_____

_____

_____

_____

_____

_____

_____

_____

_____

_____

_____

_____

_____

_____

DAY 30 - RESTING IN MARRIAGE

Marriage is so vital it is compared to Jesus' relationship with the church (Ephesians 5:23 NLT). Marriage should be restful, full of mutual support. Ecclesiastes 4:11 (NLT) says: "Two people lying close together can keep each other warm. But how can one be warm alone?" It is restful to know that the search is over; that we have a marital partner to share life with. Marriage is to be a place of rest; that is, settling down.

Yet marriage isn't always easy. That's why the vows include warnings that things may get better or worse; we may become richer or poorer, we may be in sickness or in health, but we're supposed to stick together. It says in Malachi 2:16 (NLT), "The Lord says, 'I hate divorce!'" Divorce, Jesus clarified, "was not what God had originally intended" (Matthew 19:8 NLT). Each day, we should strive to become easier to love and easier to live with (I Corinthians 13, NLT). Let's pray to make our marriages restful.

Prayer

Lord, I believe in the sanctity of marriage. I believe it is your original design for men and women and that the family is the basic unit of human society. I know that the honeymoon period ends and sometimes strife enters in. When the ups and downs of marriage and life assail me, let me look within myself rather than to my spouse to change. Let me strive to put You first, to turn to You as the source of all love. Let me work on my character to more closely resemble Your image. Soften my thoughts and my words and my ways and make me the best possible marriage partner. Let me remember that to be forgiven I need to forgive; to be shown mercy I need to have mercy. Let me take Your perspective on my marriage and on my marriage partner, and let the peace and rest of marriage begin with me. Starting now, please help me to become easier to love and easier to live with. Please give me a new and godly attitude of Christ-like love for my spouse. In Jesus' name I pray.

Devotional Notes & Scripture References

_____

_____

_____

_____

_____

_____

_____

_____

_____

_____

_____

_____

_____

_____

_____

_____

_____

_____

_____

_____

_____

_____

Devotional Notes & Scripture References

_____

_____

_____

_____

_____

_____

_____

_____

_____

_____

_____

_____

_____

_____

_____

_____

_____

_____

_____

_____

_____

_____

_____

_____

_____

DAY 31 - RESTING IN
THE OASIS OF HIS LOVE

Life can seem like a barren, desolate, desert wasteland at times. It is comforting to know that the great biblical people felt this way sometimes too. David cried out, "O God, you are my God; I earnestly search for you. My soul thirsts for you; my whole body longs for you in this parched and weary land where there is no water" (Psalm 63:1 NLT). He also said: "As the deer longs for streams of water, so I long for you, O God. I thirst for God, the living God" (Psalm 42:1-2 NLT).

The Lord wants us to have life and have it more abundantly (John 10:10 KJV). This comes from a relationship with Jesus. In John 7:38, Jesus compares himself to a well: "Anyone who believes in me may come and drink! For the Scriptures declare, 'Rivers of living water will flow from his heart'" (NLT) and "Those who drink the water I give will never be thirsty again. It becomes a fresh, bubbling spring within them, giving them eternal life" (John 4:13 NLT).

Jeremiah says without God we will be "like stunted shrubs in the desert, with no hope for the future... [We will] live in the barren wilderness, in an uninhabited salty land. But blessed are those who trust in the Lord and have made the Lord their trust and confidence. They are like trees planted along a riverbank, with roots that reach deep into the water. Such trees are not bothered by the heat or worried by long months of drought. Their leaves stay green, and they never stop producing fruit" (Jeremiah 17:6-8 NLT).

Prayer

Lord, I thirst for Your presence, love, and grace. I admit I am often in a barren, salty land where there is no water, sometimes by my own doing when I give in to the temptations of the world and the flesh. Surely this world is like a desert to You. I wish for my heart to be a constant wellspring of love, peace, grace, and joy. Let me drink at the eternal fountain of Your love and let me share that love with others wherever I go and whatever I do. Let me be like a tree planted by the living water having no fears during times of drought, because my roots are deep in the streams of the Lord. Then I will never cease or fail to bear fruit. I will live a well-watered life in the oasis of Your love and I will offer that life and love to others. In Jesus' name I pray.

Devotional Notes & Scripture References

_____

_____

_____

_____

_____

_____

_____

_____

_____

_____

_____

_____

_____

_____

_____

_____

_____

_____

_____

_____

_____

_____

_____

Devotional Notes & Scripture References

_____

_____

_____

_____

_____

_____

_____

_____

_____

_____

_____

_____

_____

_____

_____

_____

_____

_____

_____

_____

_____

_____

_____

_____

_____

HAVE A PRAISE REPORT TO SHARE
AFTER READING THIS DEVOTIONAL?

Send us your testimony at share@wellwateredlife.com
We'd love to hear from you.

ABOUT THE AUTHOR

Todd L. Shuler is an internationally known management consultant, speaker, ordained minister, teacher and author.

He brings a background of management consulting and business and IT Strategy and Implementation for both the private and public sectors, having worked for Deloitte and Ernst & Young. He also previously worked for On Assignment, Citizant, Texas Instruments, and Bank of America.

Todd graduated from the Terry College of Business at the University of Georgia with a Bachelor of Business Administration in Management Information Systems and a minor in Japanese Language and Literature. He is currently pursuing his Master of Divinity at Reformed Theological Seminary as well as his Master of Business Administration (MBA) at the J. Whitney Bunting School of Business at Georgia College and State University.

Todd is passionate about discovering the Will of God for his life as well as connecting people to God, to their purpose, and to others. He and his wife Evetta have three wonderful children.

.

OTHER BOOKS BY TODD SHULER

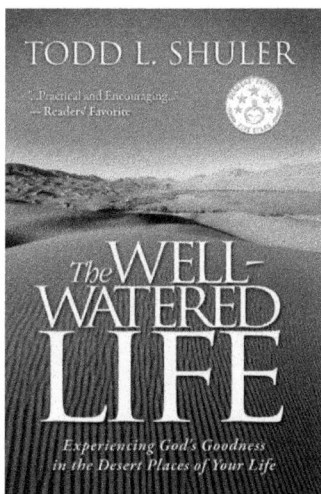